D0871319

# RUTH NEWMAN

## A LIFETIME OF ART

Seventy
Color Reproductions of Paintings

1956 - 1993

Published by John V. Newman
Westlake Village, California
1993

Published by John V. Newman
Westlake Village, California

Library of Congress Catalog Card No. 93-093702

I t is inspiring to see this record of so much of the work Ruth Newman has done over the past decades. These paintings are presented chronologically, and the evolving movement from subject to subject and medium to medium is a fascinating record of her creative growth during these years.

Her ability to capture the spirit of Mexican life with the lovely blocks of color and intriguing compositions is remarkable. *Vendedora* is especially appealing. She has used these same techniques to depict similar subjects in so many other parts of the world. Most importantly, the viewer has a good and authentic portrayal of the life of the people, the villages and the customs so important in the rural areas she has visited. In Asian painting, one of the most important qualities sought is *chi* or the essence of life. Ruth Newman's paintings certainly have this spirit.

My *Thoughts on Painting* at the end of the biography is especially interesting. We are often curious about why artists paint as they do and these comments explaining her creative process are fascinating.

Congratulations to the artist and all the family who are involved in this publication. This is a marvelous tribute to the creative talent of Ruth Newman.

Delores Bremner
Senior Docent
Pacific Asia Museum

# ACKNOWLEDGEMENTS

EDITED BY

Peter and Mary Newman

FOREWARD BY

Delores Bremner

NOTES BY

Mary Newman

REVIEWED BY

Michael J. Newman
Delores Bremner
David Newman
Gerard Shuirman
Shirl Armstrong Shuirman
Lt. Michael S. Newman
Robyn Brook

RESEARCH BY

Cynthia Stone

GRAPHIC DESIGN BY

Elsa Carl
Clarence Lee Design & Associates

PHOTOGRAPHY BY

Christopher Zsarnay
Z-Studios

PRINTED BY

Ventura Printing, Inc.

# INTRODUCTION

Ruth and John Newman,
Rancho Rio Vista, Ojai,
California.

I have always told Ruth that she should promote her art more, but she is quite shy and just isn't interested in self-promotion. She also felt that it would take all the fun out of painting if she had to think business and paint for other people's tastes. She has been featured in twelve solo shows and many people have purchased her paintings, so she has already received substantial recognition. But I am so proud of her craftsmanship and the imaginative and original approach she brings to her work that I have always felt she deserved more acclaim. When our daughter-in-law Mary, who has a master's degree in Art History, suggested that there should be a book of Ruth's paintings for our descendants to enjoy, I jumped at the idea. This volume is the result. I feel that it is a fitting tribute to a wonderful person and a very fine artist. It is also my "thank you" to someone who has been a terrific lifetime companion.

Ruth and I want very much to thank all the individuals who contributed to the production of this book. First, our family who worked so hard at making it a reality: our son Peter and his wife Mary, our son Michael, and our grandsons David and Michael. Also, our thanks to our talented friends Elsa Carl and Clarence Lee of Clarence Lee Design & Associates, Inc. in Honolulu, who were responsible for graphic design. The artistic and accomodating Chris Zsarnay of Z-Studios in Ventura did the photography, and the book was printed by the very professional people at Ventura Printing. Reviewing was very capably handled by Michael J. Newman, Delores Bremner, David Newman, Gerard Shuirman, Shirl Armstrong Shuirman, Lt. Michael S. Newman, and Robyn Brook. We would also like to thank the individuals who loaned us their paintings for the photography sessions.

John V. Newman
Westlake Village, California
September, 1993

Ruth Newman in her studio at Rancho Rio Vista, painting *Bridge on a Rainy Night*
which is in the collection of Colleen McAvoy, San Mateo, California.

Designs made in high school
art class.

California Scene
Pomona College 1930 - Oil.

**M**y memories of childhood are sharp and very pleasant. I was raised in Orange County, California, first in the city of Orange and then, starting in the fifth grade, on an orange ranch near Tustin, California. My parents, Walter and Jean Tantlinger, had six children: Helen, Jean, John, Ruth, Norma, and Keith. Our brother John was killed in a hunting accident when he was sixteen. Helen, Jean, Norma, and I all went to Pomona College and Keith studied engineering at UC Berkeley. Helen and Jean were teachers for years and married wonderful men, Rudolph "Dick" Richards and John "Ebby" Ebersole. Norma married a very nice Canadian student at Pomona College named Clarence Sorensen who went on to Harvard Business School while she finished her degree at Radcliffe College. Norma and her son David are also painters, as is Keith's daughter Susan. Our mother was a painter too, so perhaps it runs in the family. Keith and his terrific wife Wanda are now ranching, and he continues to consult after a distinguished engineering career. He gets his engineering talent from our father, who could fix anything and who was an inventor, in addition to teaching Latin and Greek in high school. He was also a college graduate, a rare thing in those days.

Even as early as four years of age, it seems I was interested in drawing. My mother made all of us practice piano for six years but this was wasted on me. She often noticed that she couldn't hear me practicing and would find me on the floor drawing pictures. My father said that when I was about four years old I would crawl up on his lap and ask if I could use his pencil. "I want to write, 'Nice Papa'" I would tell him. Of course he knew I wanted it for drawing, not for writing.

I took the school bus to Tustin Grammar School, a small but excellent school with wonderful teachers who made us really learn. I met my future husband, John Newman, in the fifth grade at Tustin. He used to bring me roses from his mother's garden near the Irvine Ranch and leave them in my desk. He also would ride his horse, Buster, over to my house to visit me. We both loved horses and riding, and we both went on to Tustin High School and then to Pomona College.

After my junior year at Pomona, I took three summer school art

Ruth with a Morgan colt at Rancho Rio Vista.

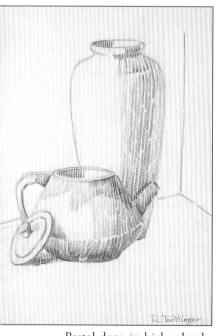

Pastel done in high school art class.

classes at UCLA which were very stimulating and enjoyable. Considering that I had taken all the available art courses at Pomona, I decided to transfer to UCLA. I changed my major from English and Psychology to Art, and took two more years and two summers of painting, crafts, design, and education courses to qualify for the Art major. My mother encouraged me to make the change and to concentrate on painting as she recognized that I was an artist at heart. I graduated from UCLA with a B.A. in Fine Arts and a teacher's certificate.

During this period, John and I enjoyed many other romances and I didn't see him much. But when we met at a Pomona reunion dance when he graduated, we knew we were a couple. I taught art for a year at Santa Ana Junior High, then we were married and I taught art in the Adult Education Department of the Santa Ana school system for eight more years. At the time, we were living and ranching on Lemon Heights. Our two sons, Peter and Michael, were conveniently born during summer vacations of that nine-year teaching period.

In 1940 John's father hired him to run a lemon ranch (the Utt Development Co., later renamed the Newman Ranch Co.) which his father and some friends had started near Oxnard. So we moved to Ventura County and lived on that ranch for eleven years. Then in 1951 we moved to a 300-acre ranch near Ojai which we had purchased in 1945. We raised lemons and cattle there for forty-three years and I raised registered Morgan horses for thirty-seven years. Meanwhile, John managed the Oxnard ranch which he continues to do even today. John has also been involved in many other business activities and he has been on a number of boards of directors. He has also been Chairman of the Irvine Company board and of the Sunkist board.

During all this time I was working in watercolor and had done literally hundreds of paintings. I took two six-week summer courses in watercolor from Eliot O'Hara at Laguna Beach, where John's parents then lived, and I took another six-week summer school watercolor course at Scripps College from Millard Sheets. I benefitted a great deal from my lessons with these highly regarded teachers. I also took watercolor and oil lessons from

Above: Ruth's solo exhibit at Danica House, Thousand Oaks, California, 1991.

Center: Ruth painting with Eliot O'Hara, 1945.

Below: Peter, Mary, and Michael J. Newman.

Theatre costume designs done at UCLA Art Department.

Design done in high school
art class.

Ruth at Rancho Rio Vista
with her painting *The Meeting*.

Phil Paradise, James Cooper Wright, Jade Fon, Jane Burnam, Dong King-
man, Gerald Brommer, Tom Nicholas, Morris Shubin, Don O'Neill, Fred
Samuelson, James Pinto, and others.

In 1955 Edith Hoffman, one of our ranch neighbors near Ojai and a
friend and patron of mine, commissioned me to paint a series of twelve
watercolor scenes. These were to be of her Rancho Casitas, where she and
her husband Walter had raised thoroughbred race horses. She wished to
record some of the beautiful views around her ranch before the Casitas
Dam was built and the house, ranch headquarters, and pastureland were
covered by water. For each painting, I would go over to the ranch in the
morning where she would show me the scene that she wanted painted
that day, and later we would discuss the painting. I loved painting for
this dear lady who treated John and me as her own children, but it
was very sad knowing that her beautiful house would soon be gone.

Then, in 1958, Edith Hoffman gave me a very interesting and challenging commission. I was to do oil paintings of the twelve California missions (out of twenty-one total) which Father Junípero Serra had named after
the stations of the cross in his hometown church. This was the Convent of
San Bernardino located in the medieval village of Petra in Mallorca, Spain
where he was born and grew up. The Church wanted to hang the paintings
next to each station of the cross, and they wanted them in a specific
size—12"x20". John and I, and our friends Kay and Bob Haley (Kay is Mrs.
Hoffman's daughter), travelled to each of these missions, spending a day at
each location. I would choose the angle I liked best and paint a watercolor
of each mission. I then painted the oils from the watercolors, and the oils
were sent to Petra. A year later, after the last hand-carved gilt frame had
been completed and the last painting hung, we and the Haleys went to see
them in their new setting. At that time, the city fathers held a dedication
ceremony and we were served a traditional *Mallorquín* lunch in the
blocked-off street outside the convent.

Some of our friends and family have since seen the paintings while
traveling in Mallorca, and I was happy to learn that they look as fresh as
ever and are now located in the entry hall instead of in the dark church. A

Edith Hoffman and Ruth at a Spanish costume party given at Mrs. Hoffman's Ventura house to view her twelve oil paintings of California missions.

Christmas card designed for Ojai's Villanova Preparatory School Scholarship Fund in the 1960's.

Tile design done at UCLA Art Department.

Right: Pewter plate that Ruth designed and made in 1938.

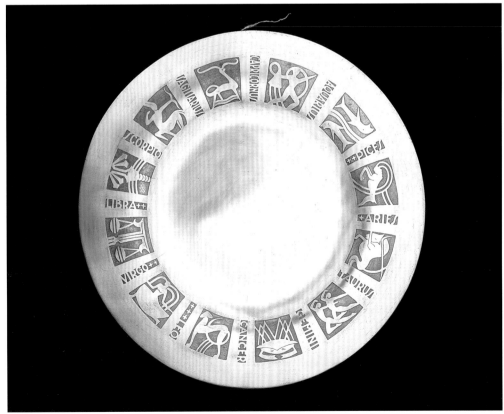

Poster made in design class at UCLA.

Ruth Newman with her painting *Bora Bora* which was used in the brochure for her solo show at Cal Lutheran College, Thousand Oaks, California in 1975.

picture in this book (p. 11) shows Edith Hoffman and me at a Spanish costume party, which she gave at her house in Ventura, to show the paintings to friends. This was just before those paintings were taken to Spain. The watercolors of the twelve missions are now hanging in the Retreat House near the Mission San Juan Bautista, California. A watercolor in this book, "Mission Montage" (PLATE 3), is a montage of all twelve missions that I painted after completing the twenty-four realistic paintings. It represented a reaction and a chance to create a more personal and imaginative impression of these missions.

In 1963 my sister Norma and I began spending each February in San Miguel de Allende in Mexico. We were taking art studies at the Instituto Allende, a branch of the University of Guanajuato. This continued for a total of eleven years, so I got quite a few credits toward a Master's degree in Fine Arts. We painted all day, every day, except for our daily hour of Spanish instruction. Initially we were painting in oil there because our American instructors were oil artists. However, in 1967 a Mexican artist came to the studio and demonstrated a revolutionary painting medium called acrylic. It was water based and dried very fast, which was a great boon to those of us who had been carrying rolled-up wet oils back home. So I, along with my instructors, switched to acrylic. At first it was a bit too much like poster paint, being thin and available only in jars. However, it soon came in tubes with a consistancy much like oil paint, and I have liked it and used it along with my watercolors ever since.

Throughout my years of painting, I have always carried a 6"x8" sketchbook and a small watercolor set with me on my travels, and many of my paintings have come from the interesting sights we have encountered on our trips around the world. I would either do a complete small watercolor on the spot or else I would sketch it in quickly in pencil, making any necessary color notes, then put on the color and complete the sketch in the hotel room that night. When I got home I was able to turn the best of these sketches into full-size paintings at my leisure. But when I have to work on a more impromptu basis—many of my best ideas have come from a brief glimpse of some passing scene or at a time when I don't have my

Ruth in President Taft's chair at the Mission Inn in Riverside, California, August 1993.

sketchbook handy–I often make a quick drawing on the back of a grocery list or other scrap of paper and then turn it into a watercolor in my sketchbook later. (Luckily I have a photographic memory.) Some of my forty-one sketchbooks are shown on pages 18-21 of this book.

I was a longtime member of the Santa Barbara Art Association, a charter member of the San Buenaventura Art Association, a member of Oxnard and Ojai art clubs and, after moving to Westlake Village in 1988, a member of the Thousand Oaks Art Association and the Art Guild of Westlake Village. I have had twelve solo shows and my works are in many private collections. I have to admit, though, that I like to keep some of my best paintings so that my family and I can continue to enjoy them.

## My Thoughts on Painting

In painting, my aim has been to interpret things in an original and inventive way; otherwise I do not feel that I am truly creating. Early on, I did many paintings that were realistic but I always left out, added, changed or moved things around to make a more pleasing composition, or I changed color schemes. Later I was not content to copy nature even with the changes. So many artists were producing so many landscapes and flower pictures that I had to paint subjects that were different, and do it my own way.

As artists gain experience, many become more interested in abstracting the subject matter or in painting purely abstract art, which means putting the composition and shapes and colors above the subject matter in importance. That's what creative art is really about: making the most beautiful shapes–both positive and negative shapes–in the most beautiful color combinations and with the most interesting composition. Subject matter can be used, or not, at the artist's will. I like to use subject matter as I think it adds another interesting facet to the painting, is a challenge to ʼ incorporate, and causes more people to relate to the painting. But in the final analysis, innovative art must come from the artist's imagination. This has been my goal and, I believe, my strength.

Ruth Tantlinger Newman
Westlake Village, California
September, 1993

Over the years a wonderful wealth of art has poured from Ruth's brushes and paintboxes! This volume portrays her evolution as a 20th-century Southern California painter from her early school projects, through her mastery of the challenges of watercolor, to vibrant oils, glowing acrylics and more. Her art is based on a strong foundation of learning from fine teachers. She has an eye for the abundance of beautiful and interesting scenery she has encountered both in Southern California and around the world. Combine these factors with her active imagination and we have the basis for the beautiful and varied canvases that delight her viewers.

Ruth's artistic talents were evident early in her life. Although she didn't go to Paris to paint and "live the bohemian life," as predicted in her high school yearbook, her early lessons with renowned teachers such as Millard Sheets and Eliot O'Hara provided her with a solid foundation of painting techniques and skills. One of the innovative founders of the California Watercolor School, Sheets and his group used full strength washes of color, one over the other, to reflect the radiant hues in California sunshine. O'Hara, too, was nationally known for his strong watercolor washes and bold brushwork. Building on this basis, Ruth's watercolors were sophisticated compositions of clear colors and strong forms that captured the look of her home state.

Many of Ruth's early watercolors are in private collections now, and some are lost, but a look into her early sketchbooks reveals charming examples of small complete watercolor paintings that are "jewels" in their own right. Reproduced in miniature on the pages of this book, we can well appreciate their spontaneous composition and fresh colors.

Ruth's art, always original and always bold, became more exciting through the years. She painted the impressionistic oil painting *San Francisco Church* (PLATE 7) for her first project at the Instituto Allende in Mexico. This was such an exciting time and setting, she remembers, that the painting "almost painted itself." Brush marks appear to fly over the canvas. Bits of white canvas show through in places. The colors are subdued compared to her later Mexican acrylics, but the brush action scattering the light and dark shades is strong and the church facade appears powerful and mysterious. This impressionistic style was repeated in her *San Miguel Hillside* (PLATE 13). In this painting, buildings the colors of sunlight are framed by a multitude of green trees until they shine against the sky like village walls in the Mediterranean sun.

During the next few years Ruth painted a wide variety of subject matter that included architecture, markets, landscapes, processions, shopkeepers, gardens, still lifes, flowers, and street scenes from her travels in Mexico and around the world. Arches, stairs, and drapery themes are repeated and, as she eliminated details and modified landscapes, she experimented with finding beauty in colored shapes. In the process, her subjects were distilled into stylized forms. The heroic figures that we saw in her 1930's UCLA costume design exercises evolved into simple colored shapes in such later pictures as *Cuatro Hermanas* (PLATE 20). Backgrounds, which were only interesting shadowy forms in earlier watercolors, now assumed importance through lively brushwork and contrasting colors.

When she exchanged her oils for acrylic paints in the 1960's, colored light and shadow became the actual subjects of her paintings as we see in *The Seance* (PLATE 33) and in *The Meeting* (PLATE 30). Individual brushmarks were no longer evident, and soon even more brilliant colors were applied smoothly, with sharp edges defining the shapes. If the painting class models wore drab clothing, she painted them dressed in glowing flat pinks, hot reds and oranges. The paintings visually vibrated with color. The backgrounds, showing no depth at all, were flat patterns in the same brilliant hues as the costumes. Colored shadow shapes were sometimes added to provide dimension, but often they were omitted. Ruth used the flat bright colors for a limited period of time. Muted colors were used in a final flat painting, *Bowling on the Green* (PLATE 43). In this painting, familiar balanced architectural forms were simplified and clarified and, against the softer colors of these forms, the anonymous players stand out in white silhouettes.

During the late 1970's, Ruth painted nostalgic still lifes, old houses, and subjects of country life such as *Spring Morning in Iowa* (PLATE 48). Her pictures during this period were "busier" and more realistic. Then, in an intellectually challenging painting, *Modern Medusa* (PLATE 61), she combined realism with an overlay of design patterns. The complexity of the patterns in *Woman from Dakar* (PLATE 51) and the shadows of the *Orange Cartons* (PLATE 50) showed her very successful blending of imagined features with reality.

Ruth's art continues to evolve in a unique direction, with the medium she uses being determined by her choice of subject matter. Her later watercolors display new concepts of texture and pattern, and include more white space than her earlier ones. Airy textures are created by painting fine lines or splashing color washes on imaginary landscapes. Colors are softer. The application of paint is freer and the surfaces show a lighter touch. Although she still is interested in her favorite subjects of light and shadow, as seen in *Our Patio* (PLATE 62), she has returned to more fancifully imaginative subjects when painting in acrylics as well. She contrasts exotic forms in *Mayan God at Tikal* (PLATE 68), shows imaginative viewpoints such as fish and legs underwater in *Koi Friends No. 2* (PLATE 67), and depicts archaic scenes in *Chac Mool at Chichén Itzá* (PLATE 69). No subject matter is against the rules.

As a teacher and fellow artist, Ruth and her paintings have influenced local artists she has known. Her art is assured, creative, witty, and she uses wonderful, magical color. Her vast reservoir of experience and knowledge allows her the freedom to turn, with great competence, in virtually any new direction she wishes. In the future, we can only wonder what exciting surprises she has in store for us! This celebration of Ruth's artistic career is especially deserved and satisfying to us all.

Mary S. Newman
September 15, 1993

18

21

PLATE 1    Ruth's Landing

Watercolor   15"x22"   1956
Collection of Jean and Robert Linnett,
Ventura, California

My friend Ruth Abernathy and I were driving home from Cambria
where we had been at a workshop taught by Phil Paradise.
We saw a little sign saying "Ruth's Landing" and decided the two Ruths
should go and see what their landing was like.
We went down a little road, found this scene, and stayed to paint it.

PLATE 2   Relic of the 1880's
Watercolor   15"x22"   1956
Collection of the artist

This is an old farmhouse in the Cambria area, where nostalgia abounds.

PLATE 3    Mission Montage
          Watercolor/Ink   15"x22"   1958
          Collection of the artist


After a commission to paint realistic watercolors and oils of twelve
California missions, I combined all twelve into one work
to create a more personal and innovative version for myself.

24

PLATE 4    Positano, Italy
Oil  20"x36"  1959
Collection of Michael J. Newman,
Big Pine Key, Florida

My sister Norma and I went with twenty Canadian painters on a painting tour:
two weeks in Paris and two weeks in Positano on the Amalfi Coast in Italy.
In Positano the houses are built on steep hills and there are stairsteps everywhere.
We stayed in a *pensione* in a setting like this painting.

PLATE 5  St. Basil's No. 1
Watercolor  22"x30"  1960
Collection of Katherine Haley,
Ventura, California

On our tour of Russia in 1959, I was intrigued by the many beautiful churches.
I did four paintings of the most famous one, St. Basil's on Red Square.
Edith Hoffman bought this one.

PLATE 6    Four Women
Watercolor  18"x24"  1961
Collection of the artist

This is one of the ideas that just came out of my head without being
triggered by anything specific. My objective was an interesting design,
and I worked it out in my sketchbook before I made the painting.

P L A T E  7    San Francisco Church
Oil  24"x36"  1963
Collection of Peter and Mary Newman,
Westlake Village, California

This was my first painting (of many!) in San Miguel de Allende, Mexico.
I was so captivated by the subject and the setting that the painting
virtually painted itself. It is one of my very favorite paintings.

PLATE 8   Watermelon Vendor
Oil   26"x36"   1963
Collection of Robert and Polly Martin,
Ojai, California

Seeing the colorful *mercados* and the Mexican people selling their
products inspired this painting. The dignity of this man added to the appeal.

PLATE 9    El Encuentro
Oil   24"x36"   1963
Collection of John Newman,
Westlake Village, California

One day in February of each year, pilgrims from many Mexican villages "encounter"
each other at a central location. They camp there, then begin walking
the next morning toward a church in San Juan de los Lagos. This trip,
taking several days, is a very colorful and impressive procession as the pilgrims
travel along with their banners, shrines, animals and camping gear.

PLATE 10   View from Spanish II
Oil   26"x36"   1964
Collection of the artist


My sister Norma and I took an hour of Spanish every day while
painting at the Instituto Allende in San Miguel de Allende, Mexico.
This was the view from our classroom window. I painted it with
no one in it in order to make it a night scene.

PLATE 11    Mercado de San Miguel
            Oil  24"x36"  1964
            Collection of Miriam Smith,
            Laguna Niguel, California

The Mexican markets have beautiful colors and shapes,
and I did many paintings of these intriguing subjects.

PLATE 12   San Antonio Church
Oil 24"x36" 1964
Collection of Michael J. Newman,
Big Pine Key, Florida

This interesting church is one of my favorites of the many in
San Miguel de Allende, Mexico. I particularly liked the details and color.

PLATE 13    San Miguel Hillside
            Oil  24"x36"  1964
            Collection of Peter and Mary Newman,
            Westlake Village, California


The Instituto Allende looks across town at this lovely
hillside in San Miguel de Allende, Mexico.

PLATE 14    Desfile del las Mujeres
Oil   24"x36"   1965
Collection of C.J. and Marilyn Schreiber,
Rancho Santa Fe, California

In Mexico, there is a yearly parade of women in colorful costumes carrying religious banners and religious objects made from straw. It's a beautiful sight.

Ruth Newman

P L A T E  1 5   Orange Vendors
Oil  24"x30"  1965
Collection of Esther and Gerry Baptiste,
Camarillo, California

Scenes like this one make Mexico very appealing to the artist.
The old colonial buildings and narrow cobblestone
streets make wonderful backgrounds for the colorful vendors.

PLATE 16    Orange Market in San Miguel
            Oil   24"x36"   1965
            Collection of Michael J. Newman,
            Big Pine Key, Florida

The big canvas canopies, umbrellas, and colors contrast with the
natives in the shadows, and the combination is irresistible.

PLATE 17     Churches of San Miguel
                 Oil    20"x24"    1965

The big Parroquia Cathedral dominates the many beautiful
churches in this lovely colonial city in Mexico.

PLATE 18   Mexican Aqueduct
             Oil   24"x30"   1965
             Collection of Peter and Mary Newman,
             Westlake Village, California


Sections of the amazing old aqueduct are visible among the tall trees and hills
on the road from Mexico City to San Miguel de Allende.
This region is the "bread basket" of Mexico, and the aqueduct
supplied water to it in colonial times.

PLATE 19    Five Faces
            Oil   22"x26"   1965

I saw a very stoic Mexican boy looking out of a window in one of
the fine old colonial houses in San Miguel de Allende. His total lack of expression
got my imagination going, so I placed comedy and tragedy
masks on each side of him for contrast.

PLATE 20   Cuatro Hermanas

Oil   24"x28"   1966
Collection of C.J. and Marilyn Schreiber,
Rancho Santa Fe, California

This painting came from a sketch made of young girls sitting
around a marketplace in Mexico. These girls do a lot of sitting, eating,
talking, and giggling as they wait for customers.

PLATE 21    Candelarias Day
Oil   28"x36"   1966
Collection of Jean and Robert Linnett,
Ventura, California

On February 2 each year (Candelarias Day), the women and children
of San Miguel de Allende, Mexico, sell the plants they have been raising all year long.
They bring these plants in tin cans, pots, cups, even in old teapots and bowls. Other entrepreneurs join
the plant sellers, setting up long tables with food and drink for sale to sellers, buyers and tourists.

42

PLATE 22   San Miguel Mirage
Oil   28"x36"   1966
Collection of Kathleen Nichols Beardsley,
Camarillo, California

This is my imaginative interpretation of the Parroquia Cathedral
in San Miguel de Allende, Mexico, and the small churches all around it.

PLATE 23    Seven Sisters
            Oil  20"x36"  1966
            Collection of Amy McAvoy,
            Camarillo, California

We were in the departure lounge at Dulles Airport waiting for a flight.
Across from us on a long bench were seven nuns who were also waiting for their flight.
The strong design created by their habits made me
(surreptitiously) get out my sketchbook.

P L A T E  2 4   Vendedora
Oil  20"x20"  1967
Collection of the artist


In Mexico, watermelon is a very popular product, almost always sold in cut pieces.
I found the girl in this scene as appealing as the melons.
This painting is one of my favorites.

Ruth Newman

PLATE 25    Sentada
Oil   18"x24"   1967
Collection of the artist

This woman and her two daughters were selling cloth
in a Mexican market. I emphasized their shapes and the
overall design with bright, contrasting colors.

PLATE 26   Monk in Bangkok
Oil   26"x30"   1967

Thailand provides many artistic combinations of colorful individuals
and interesting settings.

PLATE 27    Watermelon Flowers
            Oil   22"x26"   1967


Cut watermelons, with their combinations of bold shapes
and strong contrasting colors, are a favorite theme of mine. Here I transformed
watermelon segments into abstract flowers.

PLATE 28
Church Facade
Oil  24"x36"  1967
Collection of the artist

In this scene from Morelia, Mexico,
I applied the paint with a "dappling" technique
in order to give the painting more texture.

PLATE 29  Rima
Watercolor  22"x30"  1967

The book *Green Mansions*, which I read long ago, inspired this
painting of Rima, a girl of the forest.

PLATE 30  The Meeting
Acrylic  24"x36"  1968
Collection of the artist

We were in Haiti, visiting a wood factory, when we saw men
making salad bowls in an alley. The lattice overhead cast an eye-catching
shadow pattern on them. To improve the composition, I changed the
placement of the men so that it looked like a meeting.

PLATE 31 Five Turtles
Acrylic 24"x36" 1968
Collection of John Newman,
Westlake Village, California

This is one of John's favorites as he likes its originality.

PLATE 32   Mexican Flowers
Acrylic   28"x32"   1968


These semi-abstract flowers were the choice of Interface
(a social welfare organization) for its 1992 fund-raising card.

PLATE 33    The Seance
Acrylic   22"x36"   1968


The unlikely spark for this painting was a dark hotel room
in Mexico City, with light from the *zócalo* making odd stripes on the walls.
I put the table and people in to make it the setting for a seance.

PLATE 34    Sea Shells No. 1
            Acrylic   24"x36"   1968
            Collection of Michael J. Newman,
            Big Pine Key, Florida

My seashell collection has been the subject of several of my
paintings, of which I like this one the best.

PLATE 35   The Casbah
Acrylic   18"x40"   1968

The narrow streets of the old parts of North African towns are
truly fascinating. There are a number of casbahs; this one is in Algiers where the
Algerian freedom fighters found a refuge from the French.

Ruth Newman

PLATE 36    End of an Era
            Watercolor   15"x22"   1969
            Collection of the artist


I was driving on Fifth Street in Oxnard, California, and saw the
original Bank of A. Levy building being torn down. Some fascinating patterns
were displayed on an interior wall, so I stopped and made a sketch.

PLATE 37    Tiger Lilies
            Acrylic   20"x30"   1969

I found long ago that the intricacies of Mother Nature are often
more beautiful than anything we could invent.

PLATE 38   Canyon
Acrylic   18"x24"   1973
Collection of Peter and Mary Newman,
Westlake Village, California


The Colorado River, with its many interesting natural forms, was the starting point
for this semi-abstract painting of a deep, water-filled chasm.

PLATE 39   Cold Day on the Lake
           Acrylic   24"x36"   1973
           Collection of John Newman,
           Westlake Village, California

Even something as mundane as television can be a source of inspiration!
Something I saw on the TV screen gave me the idea for this painting.
However, I had to flesh out the concept quite a bit.

PLATE 40    Guanajuato Market
            Acrylic   24"x36"   1973


This Mexican market, in a big building with huge festoons of drapery,
was so spectacular that I could hardly wait to paint it.

PLATE 41   Each Behind His Screens
Acrylic   24"x36"   1973

A psychiatrist was saying on television that everyone
keeps part of himself from others, that "everyone lives behind his screens."
This scene popped unbidden into my mind and I quickly sketched it.

PLATE 42   Bora Bora
Acrylic  24"x36"  1975
Collection of Michael J. Newman,
Big Pine Key, Florida

We were staying in a beach hotel on this lovely fantasy island.
One morning we went down the stairs and out this door directly onto the beach.
The light and the scene were absolutely perfect, and
this is how I prefer to remember Bora Bora.

PLATE 43  Bowling on the Green
Acrylic  24"x36"  1975
Collection of the artist

In Perth, Australia, our old Victorian hotel was across from
the green and we were able to watch the very properly dressed bowlers
at their games. I liked the contrast of their all-white clothing
so much that I decided to emphasize it.

PLATE 44   Mexican Laundromat
Acrylic  20"x28"  1975

Countryside scenes like this are common wherever people and cacti
come together in Mexico.

PLATE 45    Girl Waiting
            Acrylic   18"x24"   1976
            Collection of Peter and Mary Newman,
            Westlake Village, California

The loneliness and expectations of this night bird are themes
played out over and over, all around the world.

PLATE 46    Broken Watermelon
            Acrylic  18"x24"  1976
            Collection of Russell and Betty Wade,
            Fillmore, California


Some children in San Miguel de Allende dropped a watermelon
and I wouldn't let them touch it until I could sketch it.

PLATE 47   The Painter
Watercolor  22"x30"  1976
Collection of the artist


Some very ordinary sights and a lot of imagination have
made paintings for me. Here the realistic part (the painter) is intended
to contrast with the abstract part (the background).

PLATE 48   Spring Morning in Iowa
          Acrylic  16"x20"  1976


Here I've depicted a new corn crop at an imagined location in Iowa,
the state where my father was born and grew up.

PLATE 49   Over Kansas
Acrylic   22"x30"   1977

Flying over Kansas, I saw the most interesting patterns
made by plowing, with brown soil and green crops alternating
in contour bands that wound around the low hills.

PLATE 50   Orange Cartons
            Acrylic   18"x24"   1979
            Collection of Peter and Mary Newman,
            Westlake Village, California


This is a familiar sight to me, being the wife of a citrus grower.
I liked the contrast between the sunlight and the shadows as well as
that between the round fruit and the square boxes.

PLATE 51    Woman from Dakar
            Acrylic   18"x24"   1979
            Collection of the artist

In Senegal, the woman wear fabulous bright prints in their dresses
and matching turbans. The design on this dress and turban is my own.
I love doing "patterned" paintings.

PLATE 52    The Long Room
          Acrylic   18"x24"   1979


Pure imagination produced this design – it was fun to put it all together.

PLATE 53  Red Cliffs
Watercolor  18"x24"  1985
Collection of David Newman,
Austin, Texas


Some sharply etched cliffs in Arizona inspired this semi-abstract painting.

PLATE 54    Moon over the Canyon
Watercolor   18"x24"   1985
Collection of Bank of A. Levy,
Ventura, California

Here I wanted to create an ethereal mood, such as comes once in a blue moon.

PLATE 55   Wild Oats
Watercolor  18"x24"  1985
Collection of the artist

This painting must have been channeled from my subconscious
as I had no idea where it was going when I started it. The final result,
for me, represents the essence of summer.

PLATE 56   High Country Thaw
Watercolor   18"x24"   1985
Collection of Lt. Michael S. Newman,
Coronado, California

This is an impression of snowmelt time somewhere near Golden, Colorado.

PLATE 57   Flower Spirit
Watercolor   18"x24"   1986


Here I was trying to portray the softness of flowers by means
of a soft, floating, "cameo" effect.

PLATE 5 8    Flower Power
Watercolor  18"x24"  1986


My goal in this painting was to depict the essence of a flower,
emphasized here by the muted background of abstract leaf forms.

PLATE 59  Lake Casitas

Acrylic  22"x28"  1987
Collection of John Newman,
Westlake Village, California

I painted this on the Haley ranch, adjacent to our former
Rancho Rio Vista near Ojai. When the Casitas Dam was constructed in
1956, the resulting lake inundated some beautiful farm land and resulted in
some of our property being condemned by the government.

PLATE 60 Palace in India
Acrylic 20"x24" 1987
Collection of Lt. Michael S. Newman,
Coronado, California

This is only a small section of the large Palace of the Winds
in Jaipur (Rajasthan), India. Like many of the temples in India,
this one has great detail and design.

PLATE 61   Modern Medusa
Acrylic   24"x26"   1987

This is a "patterned" painting from my imagination.
The snake-like tendrils that emanate from the girl's head
connect her to her classical counterpart.

PLATE 62   Our Patio
Watercolor   15"x22"   1988
Collection of the artist

The afternoon sun makes some interesting shadow patterns on the
patio of our home on Westlake Island, California.

PLATE 63  Cavorting Carp
Watercolor  15"x22"  1989

This is a study in color and design that I painted with no drawing or planning.
I just started putting on colors and let it evolve. One shape emerged that looked like a fish.
Once I knew that I was painting fish, I put in the other details.

PLATE 64   Wood Flowers No. 1
Watercolor   22"x30"   1990
Collection of John Newman,
Westlake Village, California

I did a series of paintings on the little flowers that grow under
the pine trees near Carmel, of which I like this one best.

PLATE 65    Chayote Vines
Watercolor   15"x22"   1990
Collection of David Newman,
Austin, Texas

I have always been a very enthusiastic gardener, surrounded by beautiful plants.
The pattern of my chayote vines – their unusual leaves, stems,
tendrils, and fruit – enticed me to paint them.

PLATE 66   Aunt Nellie Returns
Acrylic   26"x36"   1991
Collection of the artist

I was told that I was very much like my mother's sister Nellie.
Here I imagine my Aunt Nellie travelling through the cosmos to pay me a visit.

PLATE 67   Koi Friends No. 2
          Acrylic   22"x28"   1992
          Collection of John Newman,
          Westlake Village, California

It seems that everyone is painting koi fish. I wanted to paint them
in a different way. Here I visualize them as very friendly and curious beings
who like to share their pool.

PLATE 68    Mayan God at Tikal
Acrylic   18"x24"   1992

All that is left now at Tikal in Guatemala is scattered ruins.
Turkey buzzards in dead trees only add to the somber aura. But we can imagine
that a Mayan god is still there, watching over it all.

PLATE  69    Chac Mool at Chichén Itzá
Acrylic   20"x24"   1992


This statue is thought to have held the sacrificial offerings at the Mayan
city of Chichén Itzá, Mexico, now in ruins.

PLATE 70  Our Atrium
Acrylic  20"x24"  1993
Collection of the artist


The atrium of our home on Westlake Island, California, was the starting
point for these semi-abstracted plant forms.